Jonah and the Big Fish

© Copyright 1993 by Kevin Mayhew Ltd.

KEVIN MAYHEW LTD
Rattlesden Bury St Edmunds
Suffolk England
IP30 0SZ

ISBN 0 86209 360 0

Printed in Great Britain

Jonah and the Big Fish

Retold from Scripture by Kathy Singleton
and illustrated by Arthur Baker

Kevin Mayhew

Jonah lived in Israel. He was a prophet who taught the people God's messages and teachings. But he didn't always do what God wanted him to do!

One day God gave Jonah a message – a warning – for the people of Nineveh in the land of Assyria. Now Israel and Assyria were bitter enemies and the people of Nineveh were very wicked. Do you think Jonah wanted to go to his enemies?

'No, I won't do it,' he said. 'Yes, you will,' said God. 'No, I won't, said Jonah, and he made up his mind to run away from God.

He boarded a boat about to sail out of Joppa Harbour to a far-off country called Spain. 'God won't find me there,' he thought smugly to himself.

By now Jonah was very tired and he went to sleep in the ship's hold. While he was sleeping, a violent storm arose. The sky was dark and the rain lashed down; thunder rolled and lightning flashed; and the huge waves crashed down on the decks. The sailors were terrified and prayed to their own gods of clay and bronze to save them. Then they threw their cargo overboard in order to lighten the load. Still the storm raged . . .

And still Jonah slept . . . that is, until the captain saw him. 'Hoi!' shouted the captain above the storm. 'Wake up, Jonah! We're going to draw lots. Whoever gets the shortest stick is to blame for this storm.' Guess who drew the shortest stick? . . . Jonah !

Then Jonah realised that he could not run away from God. God is everywhere. 'Throw me overboard,' said Jonah, 'then God will stop the storm.'

When the sailors saw how powerful God is, they believed in Him and thanked Him for saving their lives.

The sailors didn't want Jonah to drown. But the storm got worse . . . and worse . . . and the boat was in danger of sinking. So eventually they agreed and threw Jonah over the side . . . splash! . . . and straightaway the storm stopped.

But God had not forgotten Jonah. Jonah tumbled through the water . . . down . . . down . . . down . . . he went; deeper . . . and deeper . . .until he fell into a huge, dark hole. Guess where he was? . . . inside the tummy of the biggest fish you can imagine! Jonah was sorry he had tried to run away from God and he thanked God for saving him.

After three days and nights the fish spat Jonah out onto a beach. 'Now, Jonah,' said God, 'go to Nineveh and give the people my warning.' 'Yes, Lord,' said Jonah, meekly, as he picked himself up off the beach. He knew he must obey God now, and so he started on his journey to Nineveh.

Nineveh was a big city with many tall buildings. Jonah was a little frightened, but he began to tell the people of God's warning: 'You must change your wicked ways and believe and obey God, otherwise this city will be destroyed in forty days.' The people listened, and . . .

Strangely, they believed Jonah! Even the king believed Jonah's warning.

He ordered everyone to turn from their wickedness and listen to God's teaching. All the people had to stop eating and drinking, and wear sackcloth and sit in ashes for a few days to show how sorry they were – including the king!

When God saw that the people of Nineveh were truly sorry and believed in Him, He forgave them and did not destroy their city. This made Jonah very cross – he felt so foolish! Poor Jonah: he never could learn. 'I knew you were a kind, loving God and would forgive them,' he moaned, 'that's why I didn't want to go in the first place. They are our enemies.' He was so angry, he stalked off into the desert and sat and sulked in the hot sun.

So God decided to teach Jonah another lesson. God made a plant grow up next to Jonah that night, and the leaves shielded him from the heat of the sun and the hot desert wind during the day. Jonah was very pleased to have the shade of the plant.

But, the next day . . .

God sent a worm to attack the plant, and it shrivelled up and died. Jonah was left without any shelter from the blazing sun and the burning sting of the wind. Oh, Jonah was angry that the plant had died – how thoughtless and selfish of the worm!

Then God said to Jonah: 'Why are you so angry, Jonah? This plant grew up one day and died the next day. You did nothing to make it grow but you feel sorry for it. Why should you care?' Jonah shrugged his shoulders: 'Well, it was useful to me.' 'Hmmm,' said God, 'The plant is like the city of Nineveh. Isn't it better for Me to have pity on a city full of so many people?' 'I suppose so,' said Jonah, kicking some stones. He felt rather small.

At last, Jonah understood and he was happy that God loved and cared so much about all people everywhere that He was willing to forgive them.

So he stopped sulking and started smiling as he began the journey back to Israel.

Note to Parents:
This story can be found
in the book of Jonah.